Rainforest Research Journal

Paul Mason

Crabtree Publishing Company

www.crabtreebooks.com

Author: Paul Mason
Editors: Kathy Middleton, Crystal Sikkens
Production coordinator: Ken Wright
Prepress technician: Margaret Amy Salter
Series consultant: Gill Matthews

Picture Credits:
Corbis: Frans Lanting 16
Getty Images: Time & Life Pictures/Victor Englebert 20b
Photolibrary: Robert Harding Travel/Robin Hanbury-Tenison 17
Rex Features: Apex Photo Agency 10r
Shutterstock: Cover, AridOcean 4r, Justin Blackn 10l, Ewan Chesser 22l, 22r, 23, Ecoventurestravel 13, 26t, Herbert Eisengruber 12t, Frontpage 6r, Eric Gevaert 25, Guentermanaus 4l, 6l, 8t, 8b, 26b, Eric Isselée 15, Jacek Jasinski 24r, Peter Jochems 12b, Wayne Johnson 27, LiveMan 29, Jonathan Lenz 21, Luis Louro 14l, 24l, Guzhevnikova Olga 18l, Dr. Morley Read 5, 7, 11, 20t, Ljupco Smokovski 9, Nicola Vernizzi 14r, Worldswildlifewonders 18r, 28, Michael Zysman 19

Library and Archives Canada Cataloguing in Publication

Mason, Paul, 1967-
    Rainforest research journal / Paul Mason.

(Crabtree connections)
Includes index.
ISBN 978-0-7787-9903-0 (bound).--ISBN 978-0-7787-9924-5 (pbk.)

    1. Rain forest ecology--Amazon River Region--Juvenile literature. 2. Amazon River Region--Juvenile literature. 3. Endangered ecosystems--Amazon River Region--Juvenile literature.
I. Title. II. Series: Crabtree connections

QH541.5.R27M38 2011   j577.340981'1   C2010-905296-X

Library of Congress Cataloging-in-Publication Data

Mason, Paul, 1967-
  Rainforest research journal / Paul Mason.
    p. cm. -- (Crabtree connections)
  Includes index.
  ISBN 978-0-7787-9924-5 (pbk. : alk. paper) -- ISBN 978-0-7787-99 (reinforced library binding : alk. paper)
  1. Rain forest ecology--Research--Diaries--Juvenile literature. I.
  QH541.5.R27M377 2010
  578.73409811--dc22

    2010032434

Crabtree Publishing Company

Printed in Canada/082016/WB20160708

Published in Canada
Crabtree Publishing
616 Welland Ave.
St. Catharines, Ontario
L2M 5V6

Published in the United States
Crabtree Publishing
PMB 59051
350 Fifth Avenue, 59th Floor
New York, New York 10118

CONTENTS

ASSIGNMENT AMAZON

My Diary – January 9, 2010

Great news in the mail today!
The Foundation has agreed
to pay for me to visit the
Amazon. I can start planning
my next research trip.

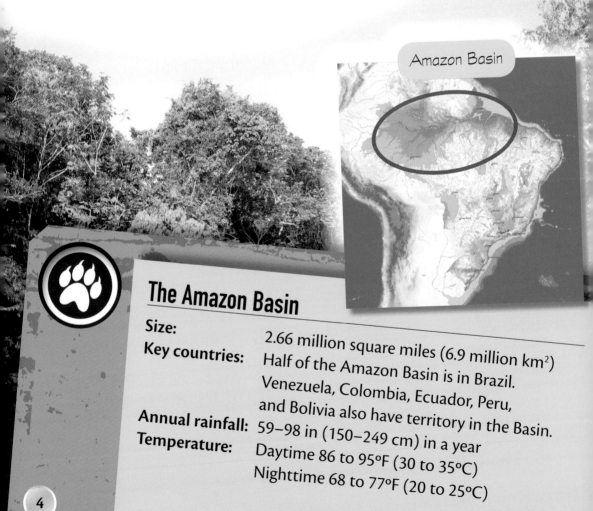

Amazon Basin

The Amazon Basin

Size:	2.66 million square miles (6.9 million km²)
Key countries:	Half of the Amazon Basin is in Brazil. Venezuela, Colombia, Ecuador, Peru, and Bolivia also have territory in the Basin.
Annual rainfall:	59–98 in (150–249 cm) in a year
Temperature:	Daytime 86 to 95°F (30 to 35°C) Nighttime 68 to 77°F (20 to 25°C)

The Foundation
1577 Overbury Road
Santa Barbara, CA
83207

The Amazon is full of animal life, such as this tree frog.

January 7, 2010

Dear Ms. Stanley,

Thank you for visiting the Foundation's offices last month.

The Directors enjoyed meeting you and hearing about your work in Borneo's rain forest. As a result, I am pleased to tell you that they have agreed to fund your visit to the Amazon.

The Foundation will use the information you provide to tell people about the Amazon's environmental problems. Please research the following:

1) We specifically wish to know how animals, plants, and people have been affected by human activity.

2) Where possible, please provide a summary of the level of **threat** they face.

The Foundation will provide you with a satellite phone to allow regular email updates on your progress.

I'd like to take this opportunity to wish you good luck with the assignment.

Yours sincerely,

Rolando Duran,
Director

TRAVELING UPRIVER

My Diary – March 11, 2010

This morning we set out upriver from Manaus. Manaus is a port city on the Amazon River. It is thousands of miles, and many days' journey, from the sea. The Amazon River is huge. Sometimes the other bank is so far away you can't see it! It will take a week to reach the Talera River.

Ruler-straight lines show where the forest's trees have been cut down.

Manaus

River Report

Name: Amazon
Length: Estimates between 3,853 and 4,225 miles (6,200 anad 6,800 km) long
Flow: 20 percent of all the river water in the world

From: Victoria Stanley [vstanley@satphoneaf.com]
Subject: Background research
Date: March 23, 2010
Time: 1:57 pm
To: Rolando Duran [rduran@thefoundation.com]

Dear Mr. Duran,

After 12 days of traveling, I have reached the Talera River. I spent some of the time researching the main threats to the Amazon. The biggest two are:

• **Deforestation**: Trees are cut down by **loggers** and by people clearing land for farming. The forest's animals and people lose their homes.

• **Pollution**: **Mining** has released poisonous **chemicals** into some rivers. The river animals and plants, and anything drinking the water, are affected.

I hope this information is useful in your campaign.

We are now traveling upstream in a small, covered canoe. I will send further reports whenever possible.

Yours sincerely,

Victoria Stanley

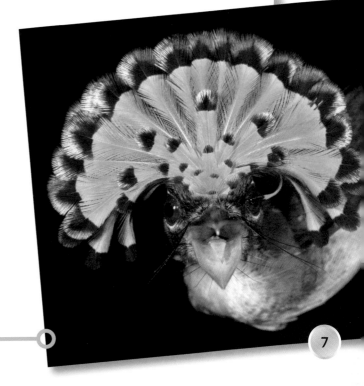

Many Amazonian animals have bright colors, like this royal flycatcher.

THE AMAZON RIVER DOLPHIN

My Diary – April 2, 2010

It's a good thing I don't mind water because we are traveling by boat, and it rains every day!

You can see the fish and other animals better here in the Talera River. The water is less cloudy. Today we even spotted some dolphins!

This Amazon river dolphin has surfaced to breathe in air.

Amazon river dolphin

Status Report

Name: Amazon river dolphin
Description: Pale gray, pink, or white, 6.6 feet (2 m) long, 264 lb (120 kg) weight
Threats: Pollution, hunting
Numbers: Classified as **vulnerable**

Bright blue
Amazonian discus
fish swim in the river.

From: Victoria Stanley [vstanley@satphoneaf.com]
Subject: River dolphins
Date: April 5, 2010
Time: 5:51 pm
To: Rolando Duran [rduran@thefoundation.com]

Dear Mr. Duran,

For the last few days we have been seeing Amazon river dolphins. These dolphins are great hunters. They catch fish and **shellfish** found at the bottom of the river.

Until recently, there were many dolphins—since they were not being hunted. The **Amazon Indians** say that killing one brings bad luck. Perhaps you could use this idea in your campaign? Now, new settlers have come to the riverbanks, and many dolphins have been caught and killed.

The dolphins are also affected by pollution. If they eat fish containing dangerous chemicals, they are slowly poisoned.

Yours sincerely,

Victoria Stanley

GIANT SPIDERS

My Diary – April 10, 2010

Tonight we are camping on the banks of the river. For dinner, we stuffed ourselves with a giant catfish that my guide caught! It's time to put up my hammock, ready for bed.

Insects are everywhere in the Amazon. This beautiful butterfly landed on my hammock!

Brazilian wandering spider

Status Report

Name: Brazilian wandering spider

Description: **Venomous**, possibly deadly, spider. Its venom causes heart and muscles to stop working. It wanders along the forest floor looking for prey.

Threats: Habitat loss

Numbers: Unconfirmed

From: Victoria Stanley [vstanley@satphoneaf.com]
Subject: River health
Date: April 11, 2010
Time: 8:20 am
To: Rolando Duran [rduran@thefoundation.com]

Dear Mr. Duran,

I have two pieces of information to report:

1) The river here appears to be in good health and unpolluted. Last night we ate a freshly caught giant catfish. The guide says that other fish are plentiful in the Talera River. I felt a little guilty eating the catfish after it just swam thousands of miles from the river's mouth to **spawn**. But we were hungry!

2) The insect life here is very rich. Before going to bed last night, we spotted a bird-eating spider dragging a snake into its burrow for dinner. And later on, something got inside my mosquito net and bit me. Fortunately, it was just a beetle and not a bird-eating spider!

It is good to see plenty of insect life because it is a sign of a healthy environment.

Yours sincerely,

Victoria Stanley

Amazonian lacewing beetles have super-sharp pincers for gripping their prey.

PIRANHA!

My Diary - April 15, 2010

As we set off this morning, our guide threw the catfish **carcass** into the river. A **school** of piranhas appeared and stripped it bare very quickly. I had been thinking about going for a swim—perhaps not!

Piranhas swim in schools for defense, not attack. You still wouldn't want them in your bath, though!

Piranha

Status Report

Name: Piranha

Description: 6–10 in (15–25 cm) long, armed with sharp teeth and an appetite for meat. Piranhas swim in schools.

Threats: Water pollution, overfishing

Numbers: Decreasing

A rare catch—a piranha that didn't bite through the fishing line!

From: Victoria Stanley [vstanley@satphoneaf.com]
Subject: Piranhas/river health
Date: April 15, 2010
Time: 6:37 pm
To: Rolando Duran [rduran@thefoundation.com]

Dear Mr. Duran,

Today we saw a large school of piranhas—further evidence that the river is not polluted. If the water was polluted there would, of course, be fewer fish. Around the world these fish are feared as fierce killers. However, they are not as deadly as many people think.

• Piranhas stay together for protection from predators, such as caimans, dolphins, and cormorants, rather than for hunting. They even eat plants as well as meat.

• There is no evidence of piranhas ever attacking and killing humans.

• Piranhas are popular food in the Amazon—despite being tricky to catch. They bite through fishing lines and nets. And if one is caught, other piranhas may eat it before it can be **landed**.

Yours sincerely,

Victoria Stanley

POISON FROGS

My Diary – April 27, 2010

Another night in hammocks!
I wandered into the forest this
evening. There, sitting in a tree,
was an amazing, bright-blue frog.
Like most brightly colored
animals, this one is poisonous,
so I didn't touch it.

Frogs love the
damp conditions
of the rain forest.

Poison-dart frog

Status Report

Name:	Poison-dart frog
Description:	0.5–2 in (1.3–5 cm) in length, brightly colored to warn off predators
Threats:	Habitat loss, chytridiomycosis (a skin disease that has affected 30 percent of the world's **amphibians**)
Numbers:	Some species are **endangered**

This black-and-white milk frog gets its name from the milky fluid that leaks from its skin when it is frightened.

From: Victoria Stanley [vstanley@satphoneaf.com]
Subject: Poison-dart frogs
Date: April 28, 2010
Time: 8:32 am
To: Rolando Duran [rduran@thefoundation.com]

Dear Mr. Duran,

Last night and this morning, I have seen poison-dart frogs in the forest. Some of these frogs are critically endangered, but they seem to be living here safely.

Researchers think some poison-dart frogs may be sources of new medicines—another good reason to protect this area.

This morning we are leaving the boat and heading west. I want to investigate rumors of jaguars nearby. Evidence that big cats live in this area could help persuade people it is worth protecting.

Yours sincerely,

Victoria Stanley

THE YANOMAMI

My Diary – April 28, 2010

Today we walked to the Yanomami village. We may see a jaguar near here, but the first thing we have seen is terrible destruction to the forest all around us.

Mining is destroying the banks of the Amazon River and causing pollution.

AMAZING FACT

Illegal gold miners are having a disastrous effect on the Amazon:

- Their high-powered hoses blast away soil from riverbanks.
- **Mercury** is used to extract gold from the soil and rock. The mercury is poisonous. It washes into the river, affecting fish, plants, and animals.

From: Victoria Stanley [vstanley@satphoneaf.com]
Subject: Yanomami Indians
Date: May 1, 2010
Time: 8:32 am
To: Rolando Duran [rduran@thefoundation.com]

Dear Mr. Duran,

I am now staying in a Yanomami village. Even here, deep in the forest, the people have heard stories about how life has changed for other Yanomami. They hear that:

• people have had to leave their land because all the trees have been cut down;

• thousands of Indians have died from new diseases brought to their lands by outsiders;

• miners have turned the rivers and streams into lifeless ditches.

They asked me if these reports are true. I said that they were, but I also said that there were powerful organizations (such as The Foundation) trying to stop the same thing from happening here.

Yours sincerely,

Victoria Stanley

These Yanomami people are dressed in traditional costumes, including bird of paradise feathers.

WAKE-UP CALL

My Diary – May 5, 2010

I was woken up at dawn this morning by a terrible shriek. At first I thought we must be under attack! Then I realized it was a macaw greeting the sunrise.

Wild macaws, like this one, are often captured and kept in cages.

Hyacinth macaw

Status Report

Name: Hyacinth macaw
Description: Largest macaw, 39 in (99 cm) long and more than 4 lb (1.8 kg) in weight
Threats: Capture for the pet trade, habitat loss
Numbers: Endangered—only 6,500 remained in the wild in 2004

From: Victoria Stanley [vstanley@satphoneaf.com]
Subject: Macaws
Date: May 8, 2010
Time: 8:32 am
To: Rolando Duran [rduran@thefoundation.com]

Dear Mr. Duran,

I have spent the last few days researching the local macaw population. These birds are familiar to people because they are often kept as pets. Unfortunately, the trade in pet macaws is one of the reasons why many species are now endangered or **extinct**.

• Over 10,000 hyacinth macaws were taken for the pet trade in the 1980s. Buying or selling them is now illegal, but the trade continues.

• Many birds have also been affected by deforestation. Not all trees have good places for them to nest, and when the trees are cut down, the birds lose their homes.

At least five species of macaw have become extinct because of the pet trade or deforestation. There seems to be a healthy population in this area of the rain forest, however.

Yours sincerely,

Victoria Stanley

This man is selling parrots that he has caught in the rain forest.

FOREST GARDENS

My Diary – May 10, 2010

One of the young girls from the village has promised to show me the tribe's rainforest garden. I've never seen one before, so I don't really know what to expect.

Cacao nuts grow in the rain forest. Chocolate is made from cacao.

AMAZING FACT

Amazon Indians have planted Brazil nut trees throughout the rain forest. The nuts are a useful source of food— they are quick and easy to eat and full of great **nutrients**.

One of the Yanomami looking after the forest garden

From: Victoria Stanley [vstanley@satphoneaf.com]
Subject: Macaws
Date: May 10, 2010
Time: 7:42 pm
To: Rolando Duran [rduran@thefoundation.com]

Dear Mr. Duran,

Today I have spent the day in the village's forest garden. It would be easy to walk past it without noticing, because it does not look like any garden we would recognize.

1) The fruits and vegetables all grow together. The Indians know which ones grow well side-by-side. This planting method means no plant takes too many nutrients from the soil.

2) After using a patch of land for a few years, the Indians leave it alone. They plant in another garden and leave the old one to recover.

3) This is different from the giant new farms in the Amazon Basin. There, single crops such as **soya beans** are grown. The nutrients are quickly used up and have to be replaced with **fertilizers**. These wash into rivers, causing pollution.

Yours sincerely,

Victoria Stanley

Watch out! This is a pitcher plant, one of the Amazon's meat-eating plants.

ON THE TRAIL OF THE JAGUAR!

My Diary – May 18, 2010, late afternoon

The villagers say that a jaguar lives in the forest near here. They have promised to take us to look for it this evening. I don't know whether to feel scared or excited! They are so rare we probably won't see one, anyway.

A jaguar uses its powerful jaws to tear apart prey.

Jaguar

Status Report

Name: Jaguar

Description: 3–6 feet (1–2 m) long, excluding tail, weight up to 297 lb (135 kg), extremely powerful Jaguars hunt mainly around dawn and sunset.

Threats: Habitat loss, hunting for skins, killed by farmers to prevent it from eating farm animals

Numbers: Near threatened, with risk of extinction in the future

This rare black jaguar is taking a nap in a tree.

From: Victoria Stanley [vstanley@satphoneaf.com]
Subject: Jaguar research
Date: May 19, 2010
Time: 9:32 am
To: Rolando Duran [rduran@thefoundation.com]

Dear Mr. Duran,

At 4:30 pm on May 18, I set out to investigate the presence of a jaguar or jaguars in the upper Talera valley. My guide was Antonio, a hunter from the village.

We set out as **dusk** was falling, since this is when jaguars prefer to hunt. We discovered evidence that jaguars do still live in the region:

1) Jaguar droppings on the trail indicated at least one large male jaguar was in the area.

2) As we followed a narrow path back toward the village, we spotted a female jaguar and her cub swimming quietly across the river.

I have photos of the female and cub swimming. These would be suitable for use in The Foundation's campaign.

Yours sincerely,

Victoria Stanley

AMAZON MONKEYS

My Diary - May 20, 2010

This morning I saw the hairiest animals of the trip so far. Up in the **canopy** above us was a group of woolly monkeys!

The uakari monkey is threatened by hunting, just like the woolly monkey.

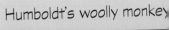
Humboldt's woolly monkey

Status Report

Name: Humboldt's woolly monkey
Description: Weight up to 22 lb (10 kg), tail used as an extra arm or leg, eats mainly fruit
Threats: Hunting, habitat loss
Numbers: Classified as vulnerable—numbers are expected to fall by at least 30 percent in the next 45 years

From: Victoria Stanley [vstanley@satphoneaf.com]
Subject: Jaguar research
Date: May 21, 2010
Time: 5:52 pm
To: Rolando Duran [rduran@thefoundation.com]

Dear Mr. Duran,

I am pleased to report some good news. We have spotted a group of woolly monkeys. As you know, this species is in danger. There are several threats to it:

1) Habitat loss—In the past, loggers **felled** large areas of forest. Today, the trees are being cleared to make way for soya **plantations**.

2) Road building—Roads cut through the monkeys' territory. This forces the monkeys to live in smaller areas.

3) Hunting—Amazon Indians have always hunted the monkeys. As new people move into the forest, more monkeys are being caught and eaten.

Our guide says that there are many groups of woolly monkeys in this area. This information should be useful in your campaign.

Yours sincerely,

Victoria Stanley

A baby emperor tamarin monkey plays with a twig.

THE FLOODED FOREST

My Diary – June 20, 2010

We have now left the Talera River and are heading for the Mamiraua flooded forest. It exists only between March and August, so I'm lucky to be here at this time of year!

Trees rise out of the flooded forest's water.

AMAZING FACT

Caimans are large animals similar to alligators. Hunting drove them almost to extinction, so the Brazilian government banned it. Now, there are so many caimans that some even live in the **sewers** of Manaus!

Caiman

From: Victoria Stanley [vstanley@satphoneaf.com]
Subject: Mamiraua forest
Date: July 10, 2010
Time: 4:09 pm
To: Rolando Duran [rduran@thefoundation.com]

Dear Mr. Duran,

We have spent the last few weeks in the Mamiraua forest, within the **reserve** there. Between March and August each year, the **water level** rises by up to 50 feet (15 m). Many trees and plants are under water. The animals have to move to the treetops or find higher ground.

The forest is home to several vulnerable species, including:

• Amazon river dolphins (see my email of April 5 for more information);

• *pirarucu*, the river's largest fish, which can weigh 440 lb (200 kg);

• black-headed uakari monkeys, which the Yanomami hunt for meat;

• harpy eagles, the largest and most powerful eagles in the Americas;

• freshwater manatees, ghostly white river creatures 10 feet (3 m) long and weighing 992 lb (450 kg).

All these animals live in the Mamiraua Reserve, where the government protects them.

Yours sincerely,

Victoria Stanley

An Amazon manatee glides through the river.

ANOTHER MISSION

My Diary – August 11, 2010

After all that time sleeping in a hammock, I'm finding it hard to get to sleep in a real bed! It must also be because I'm feeling so excited, after Mr. Duran's email yesterday. I'm just going to read it again—I still can't believe it's true.

This young three-toed sloth is climbing through the trees in search of food.

Status Report

Name: Pygmy three-toed sloth

Description: 16 in (41 cm) tall, excluding tail (tail is up to 2 in (5 cm) long); weight up to 7.5 lb (3.4 kg)

Threats: Hunting by visitors to home island, habitat loss because of tourist development

Numbers: Critically endangered

From: Rolando Duran [rduran@thefoundation.com]
Subject: Assignment Panama?
Date: August 10, 2010
Time: 8:20 am
To: Victoria Stanley [vstanley@satphoneaf.com]

Dear Victoria,

The Directors have reviewed all the information and images you sent back from the Amazon. They are extremely pleased with the work you have done.

They would like you to continue your journey. If you agree, the Directors would like you to travel to Panama. They need information about the following threatened species:

1) jaguarundi, a small wild cat—Little is known about how many of these cats there are, except that very few survive;

2) pygmy three-toed sloth—Critically endangered, it is only known to live on one small, island—3.5 miles (5.6 km) long;

3) red spider monkey—This animal is close to extinction because of logging and being hunted for food.

I hope that it is possible for you to undertake this mission. Please let me know within the next three days.

Yours sincerely,

Rolando

The tapir is one of Panama's most endangered animals.

GLOSSARY

Amazon Indians People who have lived in the Amazon rain forest for thousands of years

amphibian Land animal that breeds and becomes an adult in water, such as a frog or toad

canopy The tops of the trees

carcass Dead body of an animal, in particular an animal that is being used as food

chemicals Substances made by humans, using chemistry

deforestation Cutting down of trees so that none are left standing

dusk Time when the sun is going down and light is dim

endangered At risk of dying out forever

extinct No longer in existence anywhere in the world

felled Cut down

fertilizers Materials used to help plants grow

illegal Against the law, banned by the government

landed Reached land. In fishing, a fish has been landed when it is brought to shore.

loggers People who cut down trees in order to sell the wood

mercury Metal that is liquid at normal temperatures

mining Digging into the earth to remove substances such as coal or gold

nutrients Substances that living things need to survive and grow

plantations Large areas where single crops are grown alone

pollution Harmful substance that makes water, air, or earth impure

reserve Area of land in which animals are protected and can live safely

school Large group of fish

sewers Channels or pipes that carry waste water away from homes and other buildings

shellfish Water creatures that live inside a hard shell, such as crabs or mussels

soya beans Beans that can be used to provide food for humans or animals

spawn Lay eggs or have young

threat Possible danger

venomous Poisonous

vulnerable At risk of harm

water level Height of water in a river or lake

FURTHER INFORMATION

Web Sites

Learn more about the Amazon rain forest and other rain forests around the world at:
http://kids.mongabay.com

Discover some of the best-known animals of the rain forest at:
www.rainforestanimals.net

The home page of the International Union for the Conservation of Nature's Red List shows details of many of the world's creatures that are under threat from extinction. Find it at:
www.iucnredlist.org

Books

The Amazon: River in a Rain Forest (Rivers Around the World) by Molly Aloian. Crabtree Publishing Company (2010).

Rain Forest Extremes (Extreme Nature) by Jen Green. Crabtree Publishing Company (2009).

The Remarkable Rainforest: An Active-Learning Book for Kids, 2nd Edition by Toni Albert. Trickle Creek Books (2003).

Rainforest (Hot Topics) by Peter Riley. Scholastic (2008).

The Great Kapok Tree: A Tale Of The Amazon Rain Forest by Lynne Cherry. Sandpiper (2000).

INDEX